The Young Adult's Guide To Achieving Success

Unlocking Secrets To Early Wealth, Happiness, And Success"

Elizabeth Wagner

The Young Adult's Guide to Achieving Success

Copyright © Elizabeth Wagner, 2024.

All rights reserved. No part of this publication may be reproduced, distributed, or transmitted in any form or by any means, including photocopying, recording, or other electronic or mechanical methods, without the prior written permission of the publisher, except in the case of brief quotations embodied in critical reviews and certain other noncommercial uses permitted by copyright law.

DISCLAIMER

The information provided in this book is for general informational purposes only. While every effort has been made to ensure the accuracy of the information contained within this book, the author and publisher assume no responsibility for errors or omissions, or for damages resulting from the use of the information contained herein.

This book is sold with the understanding that the author and publisher are not engaged in rendering legal, financial, medical, or other professional advice. The reader should consult with a professional in the respective field for any such advice.

The Young Adult's Guide to Achieving Success

TABLE OF CONTENTS

CHAPTER 1

What Is The Cornerstone Of Success?

CHAPTER 2

Tips For Success At A Young Age

CHAPTER 3

Six Habits Of Highly Successful Young Adults

CHAPTER 4

Financial Literacy: Five Fundamental Ideas To Understand

CHAPTER 5

Passive Income Ideas: Ways To Build Wealth

CHAPTER 6

Education And Career: The Path To Fulfillment

CHAPTER 7

Balancing Success And Wellbeing

CHAPTER 8

Legacy Building: Building For The Future!

CHAPTER 9

The Power of Long-Term Financial Planning: Creating a Peaceful and Prosperous Future

CHAPTER 1

What Is The Cornerstone Of Success?

Do we always acknowledge success? Every person's definition of success varies. Some individuals define success based on the quantity of credentials, while others have no notion of what success means to them. Some other individuals measure success as how much money they earn or create. Others connect success with a promotion at work. Others look at their driveways and consider the automobile they drive to be a success.

I define success differently for myself. Success for me is finding pleasure inside myself without the help of others, dealing with life's ups and downs on my own, and yet gazing in the mirror and congratulating myself for the guts to change my conduct toward myself.

Accepting errors as lessons in life. What did this include? A lot! Overcoming self-doubt. Overcoming self-destructive thoughts Recognizing and appreciating my talents and flaws.

Understanding my self-worth: Discovering my principles and achieving my objectives by overcoming the restrictive assumptions I held about myself. Healing and nourishing my inner self by recognizing and realizing the genuine self. Everything boils down to self-esteem, but what exactly is it? It is how we see ourselves without any extraneous influences. How do you feel about yourself while you're doing nothing? Are you capable of doing nothing? Do you believe you have to be racing about to appreciate yourself? Do you continually feel the need to be active in anything because else you would feel worthless? What words did you hear from your parents or others as a child? Were the words you heard kind, encouraging, and inspiring, or were they unkind? Were you screamed at? Did you feel like no one had time for you?

Our experiences at an early age have a significant influence on our lives later on. Our experiences shape our views about ourselves, how we perceive the world, and, ultimately, who we feel we are at our core. The core differs from your beliefs. We create our views based on how we see the world around us, and what our parents had or did not have; their ideas are transferred onto us, and their objectives vary from yours. We often end up doing things that our parents desired for themselves.

I am fortunate in that I have always wanted to be a teacher; it was MY idea and my ambition. Nobody expected me to become a teacher, but my parents believed in me. I believed in myself since it was a deeply held ambition of mine. Was it simple to be accepted back then since there was a selection procedure in place that required you to pass specific examinations before you could begin training? It wasn't easy, but I passed. Was the training easy? In part, but not always. Did I want to give up in the middle? Yes, I did. Have I completed my training? Oh, absolutely. I worked as a teacher for 28 years. Then I was introduced to a new topic. I am still a teacher but with a different topic. Most people's childhood experiences pale in comparison to what they now teach.

Teachers nowadays are facilitators, guides, and mentors. You can only lead and coach someone willing to be led and mentored. Teachers are frequently seen as preachers. Some are; others are not. When I first began my career, I worked as a preacher because it provided me with security. With over 30 years of teaching experience, I've learned not to preach. I don't need to preach anymore. I realized that guiding is considerably more valuable than telling children what to do and what not to do.

I realized that including children in the process of learning and choosing what is good and wrong, as well as attempting to reason with them, was far more beneficial. Of course, there are fundamentals, but they should come from home. I could only attempt to make young people realize that success is determined by each person, and I would talk to my pupils freely and honestly, always telling them that I was there to help them succeed in the topic I taught, but at the end of the day, they had to do it themselves. I attempted to stimulate and urge them to succeed, telling them that their school credentials would take them to life, but they are not life, since, let's face it, life begins after school. Life begins when we have to stand on our own two feet when we have to purchase your toothpaste!

Few individuals are prepared for life, and the majority feel that if they make others happy, they will be happy themselves. This is an illusion. Many individuals believe in this delusion. This is due to poor self-esteem. Self-esteem is how you see and feel about yourself. It is your self-belief, not pleasing others. There are three basics for developing self-esteem.

Acceptance of Oneself

Accepting your talents and faults leads to self-love. Thriving/flourishing leads to personal development. If you can master them, you'll be on your way to developing self-esteem. These are the foundations of self-esteem, and if any of them are loose or weak, anything you construct or attempt to create will eventually collapse. Because you're always attempting to mend things. It resembles a shattered piece of porcelain.

You dropped it, it broke, and you repaired it. You use glue to repair it. Have you observed that after a few years, the areas where you applied the glue changed color? You can see the markings. I am sure you understand what I am talking about. You can mend some things over and over again, but there comes a point when you can't fix them anymore because they've broken too often. This is when the human body begins to mend itself. And we may seek others to see if they can help us.

Nobody can. We all have to mend ourselves. You alone know your wounds, and those wounds need to be treated, every scar you have will remind you that you repaired those wounds on your own since everyone else you believed might help you was only a bandage or a plaster covering your wounds. You can only seek individuals who can aid and lead you through your healing process, but you must do it alone in the end.

It is your duty. But we all make various decisions. We may choose to progress or to feel like a victim of life. You may choose to exercise or consume junk food and laze on the sofa all day doing nothing. Everyone has options in life. What will you choose? I am now a Transformational Mindset Therapist, and I still enjoy teaching and educating people based on my own life experiences.

Some of my experiences were truly horrendous, but once you understand and recognize that each of them had a lesson attached to them, each of which I mastered by overcoming adversity, fear of failing again, and fear of success (I can now claim successes for myself without giving them away!) I learned one important lesson: life is a choice. We pick based on our convictions. Try doing nothing for the whole day and see how you feel. It'll disclose a lot. Busy doing nothing! You might be working on your self-esteem while doing nothing. Others may see you are doing nothing, but this should not disturb you since you are aware of your hectic schedule.

CHAPTER 2

Tips For Success At A Young Age

Become a youthful success and enjoy the benefits as an adult. I will provide you with the necessary skills to make it happen. It would be wise for you to begin preparing for success at an early age.

Here are some strategies to help you achieve success at an early age:

Surround yourself with like-minded individuals. Improve your time management abilities. Adopt a lifelong learning attitude. Accept errors and failures. Network Stay disciplined. Maintain both your physical and mental wellness.

Surround yourself with like-minded people. The people you spend time with have a significant impact on who you become. Surround yourself with individuals who are enthusiastic about what they do. Receiving advice and views from those who are unwilling to put in the effort will not benefit you. Surround yourself with individuals who share your goals, want to succeed, and are ready to work hard. This allows you to be driven by your pals while also motivating them.

Improve your time management. Time management skills are vital for success in everything you undertake. Learning to manage your time wisely and successfully at an early age can help you achieve success in the future.

Adopt a Lifelong Learning Mentality. Being successful requires a solid educational base. Obtaining a certification in an area that you are enthusiastic about is critical since you will not lose interest. Educate yourself by reading books that are relevant to your credentials or that motivate you to remain focused.

Accept your mistakes and failures. Everyone fails and makes errors; some of the most brilliant minds we know today failed or made a mistake at some time in their lives. It's all about trial and error; you won't know what works and what doesn't until you're ready to fail. Accept your shortcomings and errors, and then use them to your benefit.

Network. Learning about networking when you are young can substantially assist you when you join the workforce. Making professional relationships at an early age can help you get a career when you need one.

Stay disciplined. Staying disciplined is essential. It's simple to slip off course, but regaining your desire may be challenging. Staying disciplined guarantees that you do not lose whatever progress you have achieved. **Maintain Your Physical and Mental Health.** Remember to prioritize your emotional and physical health. There are several actions you may take to assist you become successful at a young age, all of which are incredibly tough undertakings to do at such a young age. As a result, getting adequate sleep is critical, since sleep deprivation has an impact on your mood.

Getting adequate physical exercise might help alleviate stress and despair. Is it better to be successful young than to become successful later in life? When you're young, you have more space to make errors and a greater tolerance for risk. The older you become, the less adventurous you get because you risk beginning again, which is frightening as you get older. Older company owners are often more informed than younger proprietors owing to their experience level.

This lack of expertise and experience may dissuade some investors. You may argue that it doesn't matter when you achieve success, but it is also worth noting that beginning early will only help you in the long term.

Why is it so important to be successful while you are young?

Most people would state that they wished they had begun working on their achievement when they were younger. Here are some of the reasons why being successful when young is important: Being successful at an early age makes you less inclined to settle for anything less later in life. If you start while you're young, you won't have to spend your whole career striving for success and accomplishing your goals. You may concentrate on your family or enjoy the results of your labor. You will discover what it means to be responsible and disciplined from a young age. A failed circumstance will be simpler for you to recover from. You will be financially comfortable by the time you reach adulthood.

What Does Being Successful Mean?

In general, success is described as being affluent or renowned; nevertheless, the success of others should not be used to assess your own.

Each individual has their notion of success. If you create objectives and accomplish them, you are successful. For example, if you aim to get a qualification and you finish your course, you have succeeded. Your next objective should always be higher than the one before it, so that you may continue to develop and succeed. What Is the First Key To Success? The first step towards success is to train oneself in new skills or get a certificate.

The Young Adult's Guide to Achieving Success

CHAPTER 3

Six Habits Of Highly Successful Young Adults

Successful young folks have accomplished their objectives and aspirations at an early age. They are determined and focused and understand how to make the most use of their time. In this section, we will look at the six habits of extremely successful young people and how to integrate them into your own life. By the conclusion of this section, you will have practical ideas for increasing your productivity, achieving your objectives, and being a successful young adult.

Set goals and prioritize. Setting objectives and prioritizing work are important habits for young adults to adopt early on. Having a clear vision of what you want to accomplish and a plan for getting there will help you remain focused and motivated.

To develop successful goals, begin by identifying your long-term objectives and breaking them down into smaller, more manageable tasks. Write down your objectives and keep them visible to remind yourself of what you're striving for. Prioritize tasks by identifying which activities will have the greatest influence on accomplishing your objectives and focusing on them first. Successful young people who prioritize and create objectives often have a good knowledge of their values, which they utilize to drive their actions. Take the time to focus on what is most important to you and use it to guide your goal-setting process. Do not be hesitant to change your objectives as needed, and remember that progress, not perfection, is the aim.

Some practical time management suggestions include scheduling your time using a planner or calendar, breaking down big activities into smaller, more manageable ones, and adopting productivity tools such as the Pomodoro method.

Successful young people maintain focus and progress toward their goals by prioritizing and creating goals. Take the time to define success for yourself, and then establish objectives appropriately. Stay focused on your objectives and remember that each step forward puts you closer to your vision.

Practice mindfulness and self-care. It's no secret that early adulthood can be stressful and demanding. That is why it is critical to emphasize mindfulness and self-care to maintain mental and physical wellness. Taking time to care for oneself may boost productivity and avoid burnout. One method to bring mindfulness and self-care into everyday living is to concentrate on breathing and being present in the moment. This may be accomplished by meditation, deep breathing exercises, or a simple stroll outdoors. Another method is to schedule time for hobbies or activities that offer you pleasure and relaxation, such as yoga, drawing, or reading a book.

Practicing self-care entails taking care of your physical well-being. This includes getting adequate sleep, being hydrated, and doing regular exercise. It's essential to remember that self-care looks different for everyone, so figure out what works best for you and prioritize it in your daily routine.

Successful young people recognize the value of self-care, both physically and psychologically. Simone Biles, an Olympic gold champion, promotes self-care by decompressing and practicing mindfulness after games. These activities help her remain focused and on top of her game. Incorporating mindfulness and self-care into your daily routine may help you decrease stress, boost productivity, and live a happier, healthier life. Don't forget to take care of yourself, since your health is critical to your success.

Continuous Learning and Personal Development
Continuous learning and personal growth are essential for success as a young adult. In today's fast-changing

world, it is critical to stay current on the newest trends, technology, and breakthroughs. Young people may differentiate themselves by constantly learning and acquiring new abilities. To create a growth mentality, young individuals should be open to new experiences, accept difficulties, and seek criticism. They should see errors and failures as chances to learn and develop, not as setbacks.

There are several methods to seek out chances for learning and growth, including attending conferences, taking classes, reading books, and networking with people in their industry. They may also benefit from professional groups or mentoring programs, which provide useful insights and direction.

Elon Musk is a successful young adult who emphasizes constant learning. He has always been interested in science and technology and has pursued a career as an entrepreneur. He is continually looking for new challenges and chances to learn and improve, such as starting SpaceX and Tesla.

Young people who prioritize continual learning and personal growth may improve their abilities, remain ahead of the curve, and accomplish their objectives. It requires devotion and hard effort, but the benefits are worthwhile.

Creating Strong Relationships. It's commonly stated that no one is an island, and that includes very successful young people. Building great connections with people is critical for personal and professional development. One of the keys to developing great connections is being deliberate and consistent in your interactions with people. This entails making time for the people in your life, being present in discussions, and actively listening to what they have to say.

Another crucial part of developing healthy connections is valuing mutual respect and compassion. This entails treating others with the same dignity and care that you would expect for yourself. It's also crucial to recognize that developing good connections requires time and effort. It is not something that develops immediately, but rather something that is nurtured by persistent effort and mutual involvement. Successful young people recognize the importance of developing solid connections, both emotionally and professionally.

They emphasize their relationships, making time for the people in their lives and actively striving to keep them. In doing so, individuals build a network of support that allows them to flourish in all parts of their lives. Take the time to invest in your existing and new connections. Reach out to friends and family, attend networking events, and look for ways to interact with people.

Building solid connections will not only help you develop personally and professionally, but it will also improve your life in numerous other ways.

Embrace failure and persevere. Despite our best efforts, setbacks and disappointments are unavoidable in life. However, how we manage these setbacks may make all the difference. Successful young individuals recognize the value of accepting failure and utilizing it as a learning experience.

One of the most crucial things to remember is to have a development attitude instead of a fixed one. This entails seeing failure as an opportunity to learn and grow, rather than a personal defect or restriction. It's also critical to maintain resilience and persistence in the face of adversity, rather than giving up at the first hint of trouble.

To recover from failure and endure hardships, keep these things in mind:

- Reframe failure as an opportunity for development and learning.
- Stay cheerful and concentrate on the positives rather than the problems.
- Use failure as an incentive to strive harder and smarter toward your objectives.

- Seek help from mentors or a solid support system.
- Take care of yourself physically, intellectually, and emotionally so that you have the strength to persevere.

Remember that failure is not a sign of weakness, but rather a normal part of the learning process. Continue to press ahead, have a good attitude, and believe in yourself.

Real-life examples of successful young people who have overcome failure include J.K. Rowling, who was rejected by many publishers before Harry Potter was approved, and Michael Jordan, who was cut from his high school basketball team before becoming a basketball superstar.

You may do great things and realize your full potential if you embrace failure and persevere through adversity.

Give back and contribute to society. Giving back and giving to society is an important part of personal development and satisfaction. It not only benefits others, but it also gives people a feeling of purpose and meaning in their lives.

Here are some particular techniques for discovering ways to volunteer and have a good impact:

Begin by defining your hobbies and passions. What are the most important reasons for you? Are there any unique abilities or talents you can offer? Make a list of organizations or activities that match your interests and talents. Discover local NGOs or charities that share your beliefs and interests. Attend their events, study their material, and get to know their employees and volunteers. Consider volunteering for a short project or event to get a sense of their work. Check with your company, school, or religious group to see if they offer any volunteer programs or projects.

Many organizations provide time off or community service days to their workers or members. Look for virtual volunteer jobs that may be completed from anywhere with an internet connection. Many organizations need help with website design, social media management, grant writing, and other work that may be completed remotely.

Don't underestimate the impact of simple acts of kindness. A smile, a kind word, or a helpful hand may significantly improve someone's day. Remember that giving back involves more than simply providing money or effort. It is about having a good effect on the world around you, no matter how large or tiny.

Finding methods to give to society may help you develop a feeling of purpose and satisfaction while also making a difference in the lives of others. Highly successful young people often exhibit similar patterns that lead to their success. These habits include setting and achieving goals consistently, cultivating a positive mindset and attitude, practicing mindfulness and self-care, constantly learning and developing new skills, forming strong relationships, accepting failure as a learning opportunity, and contributing to society.

To become a successful young adult, you must take action and incorporate these habits into your everyday life. Begin by establishing clear objectives and making a strategy to attain them, concentrating on a development mindset, and prioritizing your physical and emotional well-being via mindfulness and self-care techniques.

Seek chances for learning and personal growth, form good connections with others, and be resilient in the face of failure. Consider contributing to society by offering your time and abilities to make a good difference in your town. By constantly practicing these behaviors, you may improve your chances of success and reach your full potential.

Remember that developing good habits is a continuous process that involves commitment and effort. By making a concerted effort to adopt these habits into your daily routine, you may position yourself for success and live a satisfying life.

CHAPTER 4

Financial Literacy: Five Fundamental Ideas To Understand

Personal finance encompasses a wide range of activities. Perhaps you are new to handling your funds. Perhaps you are taking on additional financial duties. Perhaps you just want to renew yourself. Whatever the situation, it may be difficult to know where to begin or how to guarantee you are making the proper decisions.

Budgeting, credit building and improvement, saving, borrowing and debt repayment, and investing are all examples of financial literacy principles. Increasing your financial literacy may make loan, large purchase, and investment choices easier.

There are several resources available for learning more about money, but it is important to seek out reliable ones.

What is financial literacy?

Budgeting, credit building and improvement, saving, borrowing and repaying debt, and investing are all examples of financial literacy ideas that may be used in real-life circumstances. If financial well-being is your objective, financial literacy might be the first step toward getting there.

Becoming financially literate entails studying fundamental ideas that will enable you to make better financial choices and achieve your financial objectives. There is no incorrect moment to work on improving your financial literacy, and there is always something new to learn about personal money.

The more financially knowledgeable you become, the more likely you are to adopt activities that will eventually lead to financial well-being. The five aspects of financial literacy There's a lot to learn about personal finance, but breaking it down may help simplify things.

Consider the following five areas to begin growing your financial literacy: budgeting, credit development and improvement, saving, borrowing and debt repayment, and investing.

1. Budgeting. Learning good spending habits is an important first step in improving your financial literacy. One method to do this is to learn to budget. You may start by defining monthly costs to include in your budget, which will allow you to monitor your spending. Budgeting might assist you avoid splurging on nonessential items. Furthermore, minimizing

unnecessary spending will free up more money for necessities and savings. There are several ways to budget, including The 50/20-30 method: This strategy entails allocating 50% of your take-home pay for necessities, 30% for desires, and 20% for savings. The zero-based method: Monthly costs and savings are deducted from your take-home pay until they reach zero, ensuring that every dollar is spent with purpose. The envelope approach categorizes all of your monthly costs and allocates specific amounts of your take-home pay to each area in real or digital envelopes.

2. Establishing and improving credit. Your credit ratings influence many aspects of your financial life. Among other crucial choices, your credit score has a big influence on your ability to purchase a home, lease a vehicle, and apply for a credit card. That's why understanding where your credit stands—and what measures you can take to improve it—is so crucial.

Understanding what influences your credit ratings may help you gradually create a healthy credit history and a good credit score. However, there are still steps you may do to raise your score quicker. Apply for just the credit you need. Understand how closing credit cards might impact the duration of your credit history. Keep your credit usage ratio at 30% or below, as advised by the Consumer Financial Protection Bureau (CFPB). Check your credit reports for inaccuracies regularly, and keep an eye on your credit scores for changes. Monitor your debt-to-income (DTI) ratio. Generally, lenders like DTI rates between 28% and 36%. The higher your creditworthiness, the more likely you are to acquire favorable conditions and lower interest rates on credit cards and other loans.

3. Saving is a crucial part of financial literacy. There are several methods to save, including standard savings accounts, retirement savings plans, investment portfolios, and emergency reserves. It might be beneficial to carefully outline your savings objectives so that you understand how much you'll need to set away. Managing bills and other obligations simultaneously might make saving seem tough. However, there are methods to save money while repaying debt.

4. Borrowing and repaying debt At some time in your life, you will most likely need to borrow money and incur debt to attain a personal or financial goal or necessity, such as attending college or renovating your house.

Personal loans, mortgages, and vehicle loans may all influence your credit and financial condition by increasing the amount of debt you owe at any one moment. And the more loans you have, the more you'll have to pay your bills each month. However, those same loans may help you buy products that would otherwise be prohibitively expensive. Credit cards are another kind of debt that may assist with more than simply daily needs. A credit card may help you develop credit if used responsibly. This includes paying your account balance on time every month and keeping track of your credit usage. Understanding the effect of debt on your finances, as well as developing a realistic strategy for paying off that debt and paying it on time, are critical components of financial literacy.

5. Investing Once you've mastered budgeting, credit, savings, and debt management, it's a good idea to start learning about other strategies to generate wealth and prepare for retirement. Learning about stocks, bonds, mutual funds, and other investment alternatives might be a good starting point. However, it is crucial to realize that investing is risky.

The amount of risk and reward varies depending on the investment. Why is financial literacy important? You'll be better equipped to make key financial choices if you understand how they'll affect your present and future financial circumstances. This may help you achieve your objectives, save money, and prevent or navigate future financial setbacks.

The Young Adult's Guide to Achieving Success

Benefits of Financial Literacy

Now that you understand why financial literacy is important, let's look at how it can directly benefit you:

It may help you prepare for crises. When you are financially educated, you may be able to better analyze your requirements and prepare for worst-case circumstances. This understanding may assist you in building emergency funds so that you can cope with financial stress without depending entirely on loans and credit cards. It may help you manage your debt more successfully. Financial literacy may help you understand how each of your loans will affect your money in the short and long run. This might make debt management simpler and allow you to prioritize payments, reducing financial burden in the long run.

It may help you achieve your goals: Financial literacy allows you to be completely aware of your status and how certain money actions may affect your finances in the future. This may help you achieve your objectives and remain motivated as you work toward them via your financial planning efforts.

It may enhance your financial habits. Overspending may be a serious issue for many individuals. But if you're financially educated, you'll understand exactly how overspending will affect your money. This might help you change your spending patterns, allowing you to better manage your debt and save for the future. How to develop financial literacy. Personal finance is an ever-changing landscape. Making financial literacy a lifetime effort may keep you informed and on track for financial success.

As you begin to educate yourself on these personal finance subjects to become more financially literate, it is important to choose your informative resources wisely.

Here are some areas you may start:

MyMoney.gov: A financial education website established by the United States Department of the Treasury's

Financial Literacy and Education Commission. Consumer education is a feature of the CFPB website that offers readers tools and information to help them make better financial choices.

Investor.gov is a website designed by the US Securities and Exchange Commission to assist readers learn more about how to invest and safeguard their interests.

Consumer advice: The Federal Trade Commission built a website to assist readers in understanding how to report fraud, prevent scams, and educate themselves about money.

Learn & Grow: A component of Capital One's website that provides useful content especially designed to assist readers develop a better grasp of a broad array of personal financial subjects. Financial literacy, in a nutshell, Developing financial literacy is a crucial component of managing money and achieving financial objectives. There are basic actions you can take to improve your financial knowledge and confidently implement what you've learned.

CHAPTER 5

Passive Income Ideas: Ways To Build Wealth

Passive income might help you earn revenue more readily after making an initial investment. Passive revenue originates from ventures that may demand some initial effort but may generate money with little to no maintenance.

Developing several passive income sources might be a creative side activity that generates extra revenue.

1. Consider purchasing index ETFs. Index funds are portfolios of assets, such as stocks or bonds, that are meant to replicate a given financial market. Index funds may help you diversify and, in certain cases, guard against loss; the more stocks and bonds you hold, the more likely you are to have winners.

Pro: Passive index funds, which are not actively managed, often have cheaper costs.

Con: Investing has inherent risks.

2. Evaluate high-dividend stocks. High-dividend stocks might be a good place to start if you want to invest.

High-yield dividend stocks often provide a greater yield than the benchmark average. This sort of investment may provide bigger returns, but it is hazardous. If you are considering this option, be sure to read the tiny print.

Pro: High-dividend investments may provide a larger dividend rate than usual. This might help supplement your annual income.

Con: There are investing hazards.

3. Research money market investing funds. Money market investment funds are a low-risk alternative to investing directly in the stock market. The purpose of this investment is to make money via interest. These investments may be backed by top-tier corporate or bank securities.

Pro: These investments are generally lower risk and may be liquidated more readily.

Cons: Earnings may be modest.

4. Pay Off some debt. You might potentially produce passive revenue by making greater payments on your existing loans. You might wind up paying hundreds, if not thousands, of dollars in interest on your debt over time. If you're searching for new investments, think about paying off your debt first.

Pro: Managing your debt may help you develop credit and free up your budget.

Con: You're not exactly generating money; you're conserving it over time.

5. Evaluate real estate prospects. If you're ready to settle down in one location, purchasing a house can be worth considering. Purchasing a house enables you to make monthly payments on an investment that may yield you money if you sell it in the future. The average property value has increased by 4.3% since 1991, according to the Federal Housing Finance Agency.

Pro: Your house investment may increase in value over time as you collect home equity.

Con: You may be responsible for more care and repairs than if you rented your living space. Furthermore, your home's worth may not always grow.

6. Consider peer-to-peer lending. If buying a property isn't an option, try peer-to-peer financing. Peer-to-peer lending occurs when you provide a loan to another individual, often via a lending platform. As an investor, you may also opt to deal directly with firms or individuals seeking money. They may make you a

monthly payment with interest without going via a banking institution.

Pro: Potential investment gains.

Con: Investment risks - if you're not utilizing a lending platform, be sure you have a documented contract.

7. Consider renting out unused space. When you're traveling, you may not utilize your house or apartment as often as you typically would. Instead of leaving it vacant, try renting out your underutilized space to generate a second income. Several internet services enable you to post your house for rent.

Pro: You have the freedom to list and limit rental dates as needed.

Con: It may take some time and effort to understand and develop reliable short-term renters.

8. Contribute to a high-yield savings account. If you're new to investing, you may want to start basic. Consider investing in a high-yield savings account.

This enables you to earn above-average interest on your deposits.

Pro: You may have the liberty to donate as much as you like and withdraw as needed.

Con: As with other low-risk investing alternatives, the profits may be smaller than others. Open a high-yield savings account with Credit Karma MoneyTM Savings.

9. Use cash-back incentives. If you can make your monthly payments on time and in full, check into several cash back rewards cards. Cashback reward cards offer you a portion of your purchases back over time. This may be an appropriate alternative for those who do not have a lot of time or money to invest straight away.

Pro: Some cash-back cards provide sign-up incentives that may boost your profits.

Con: If you do not pay your balance in full each month, you will often incur interest, which may negate any cash-back incentives. Unlock your net worth. Get started.

10. Use affiliate marketing. If you have an entrepreneurial spirit, you may pursue affiliate marketing. Affiliate marketing allows you to earn a portion of the items or services you suggest. For example, if you have a large number of followers on your blog, discuss items or services you like. While

doing so, sign up for affiliate marketing services to develop personalized links. If you click on the links and make a purchase, your commission earnings may grow.

Pro: These links are typically active for the duration of your article. Even if you publish these purchases years later, you might still make money.

Con: Your profits are not assured. If you have a large number of followers, you may be able to earn extra commissions.

11. Take stock photos to sell online. Consider turning your hobby into a passive source of money. If you like going out on weekends to snap images and films, try selling them online. That way, individuals looking for fresh stock pictures and videos may discover and utilize your assets. In addition, you may sell these photographs for as long as they are online.

Pro: If you have a large collection of photographs or films, you may be able to make money from a "passion" project.

Con: Some stock picture companies impose commission rates and other costs for selling your work on their platform.

12. Create and sell an e-book. If you have a tale to tell or a skill to give, creating an eBook is an excellent method to generate passive money. For example, you might build a fitness eBook with a list of all your favorite workouts. Just bear in mind that you may need to continuously re-promote your items to reach individuals who have not yet seen them. Pro: You have total control over your narrative, messaging, and price. Con: If you don't have a big and dedicated following, sales may take longer to materialize.

13. Offer products for sale online. Over time, there may be goods that you no longer use but know still have monetary worth. You may sell these products on eBay, Amazon, Poshmark, and other marketplaces. The negative is that you may need more maintenance than other passive income alternatives.

Pro: You can offer anything for sale, whenever you want, and at whatever price you want.

Con: Depending on the seller platform you pick, you may be charged seller fees or commission rates.

14. Create an application. For tech-savvy creatives wishing to generate passive income, developing an app might be the way to go. If you've seen an opening in the app market throughout the years, you may already have

an idea of what you want to build. With a limitless supply of video lessons and study manuals available online, you may have all the necessary materials right at your fingertips.

Pro: You can invest with only a few clicks of a button. Plus, you have complete control over your invention and its listing price.

Con: You may have to face a high learning curve. Not to mention that creating that curve may need a significant amount of work upfront.

15. Create an online course. Creating an online course, like writing an eBook, is an excellent way to generate passive income. If you have mastered specific talents, this might be an excellent opportunity to display them. You might design an online course on any subject you choose, from blogging to beginning a side business.

Pro: You may utilize your power in a specific location and have complete control over the creation and selling value.

Con: Once again, there may be a significant learning curve. Not to mention the significant upfront time required to present your finest work.

16. Design and sell T-shirts. If you like photographing or making distinctive designs, try putting them on T-shirts and selling them. Several sites enable creatives to publish and sell their artwork. Consider getting the necessary components to create your own. Once you've added your artistic touch, sell them online to potentially earn from a pastime. Pro: This may be a fun and innovative method to build up your passive income over time. Con: You may have to cover the initial price of obtaining your supplies. Along with that, you will suffer the price of outsourcing operations and must deal with maintenance.

17. Start a blog. Creating your website might lead to a variety of passive income opportunities. You may start a blog, grow your following, and raise your revenue via sales. You could make your eBook, online course, or even design T-shirts and sell them all on one platform. Pro: Building a website requires a relatively cheap initial cost.

Furthermore, depending on your design, it may be completed in as little as a few hours or days.

Cons: Online systems demand consistency and upgrades. Not to mention, your following will not grow overnight.

18. Sell designs online. If you have graphic design abilities, you might use them to earn a passive income by developing Canva templates or selling designs on Etsy. As a Canva contributor, you may sell your licensed pictures, graphics, stickers, or movies and make money from Canva users who utilize your works. Etsy also enables you to set up a shop and sell your creative creations online.

Pro: You may select how much time you want to devote to it and utilize it as a creative outlet while still earning a passive income.

Con: If you aren't already generating these designs for personal use or fun, it may seem time-consuming with little to no payback if your designs don't sell quickly or aren't picked by customers.

CHAPTER 6

Education And Career: The Path To Fulfillment

The transition from college to work might seem like traversing a wide and unknown landscape. We're inundated with inquiries like, "What should I study?" Which job route matches my interests? How can I bridge the gap between the classroom and the outside world? But do not worry, intrepid adventurer!

This section will help you navigate the complex world of school and job options.

Charting Your Course: Discovering Your Passion The first step in every successful trip is understanding where you're going. So how do you find your passion? Self-reflection is essential. Think about your strengths, hobbies, and values. What topics excite you? What hobbies get you curious? What issues do you want to solve? Don't be hesitant to try new things, volunteer in other professions, and even shadow pros to obtain direct knowledge. Remember that your passion does not have to be a single thing; it may be a collection of hobbies that lead you to a rewarding profession.

Education: Your Launchpad Once you've found your passion, education is your rocket fuel. However, the "ideal" educational route is not necessarily a straight line. Consider conventional education alternatives such as universities and colleges, as well as vocational training, apprenticeships, and online courses. The goal is to pick an educational route that will provide you with the skills and information you need to succeed in your chosen industry. Remember that education is a lifetime endeavor, therefore embrace ongoing learning and development throughout your career.

Building Your Skill Set: Beyond the Degree While formal education gives a solid foundation, the actual world requires a wide skill set. Improve your communication, collaboration, and critical thinking abilities. Improve your problem-solving talents and learn to adapt to shifting surroundings. Embrace technology and remain current with industry developments. Remember that soft skills are frequently equally as vital as technical talents, so don't overlook their development.

Networking: Your Guiding Light Your network serves as your professional compass. Connect with mentors, industry experts, and other job seekers. Attend conferences, seminars, and industry-related activities. Develop genuine connections and don't be afraid to seek help and assistance. Remember that your network is more than simply who you know; it also includes who knows you. The journey is the reward, so accept flexibility and progress. Your job path will not always follow a straight line. Be open to new chances, unexpected twists, and even brief diversions. Accept lifelong learning and constant development.

Remember that success is more than simply getting to your objective; it's also about enjoying the ride. So, approach your work with passion, dedication, and a desire to learn and adapt. The transition from school to work is an exciting and changing experience.

Understanding your interests, equipping yourself with the necessary abilities, and embracing continual learning can help you navigate this complex terrain and establish a meaningful future. Remember that there is no one-size-fits-all method; each trip is unique. So, design your path, accept the unknown, and never stop exploring. The world is eagerly awaiting your abilities and efforts. Now, make your mark!

CHAPTER 7

Balancing Success And Wellbeing

As you are aware, a truly rewarding career is defined by more than just financial success; it also includes your overall well-being, so I believe we should discuss the art of maintaining work-life balance, including tips for prioritizing self-care, setting boundaries, and celebrating your career accomplishments.

I prefer the word 'harmony' instead of 'balance' because balance implies that there are only two things: work and life. That is it. I think there are four things you can balance in your life if you want to feel less stressed, more grounded, and simply more like yourself:

Physical Health: Begin by emphasizing your physical health. Regular exercise, a balanced diet, and proper sleep are the foundations of good health. Make time for physical exercise, eat nutritional meals, and obtain enough restorative sleep. Your mental health is vital. Practice stress-reduction practices including mindfulness, meditation, and deep breathing exercises.

Seek help from a mental health professional if necessary, since maintaining your mental health is an important element of self-care. Time Management: Proper time management may considerably minimize stress. Calendars, to-do lists, and productivity applications may help you manage your responsibilities and schedule time for relaxation and leisure activities.

Hobbies & Interests: Make time for activities that provide you pleasure and relaxation. Reading, drawing, playing a musical instrument, or gardening are all enjoyable hobbies that are beneficial to your overall health.

Unplug from technology. Schedule "tech-free" time to disengage from screens and digital gadgets. Constant connectedness may cause fatigue, therefore it's critical to set limits with technology.

Designate workstation: If you work remotely or have a flexible schedule, set up a dedicated workstation away from your living quarters.

This physical wall contributes to a distinct division between work and personal life.

Work Hours: Set certain work hours and adhere to them as closely as feasible. Communicate your working hours with coworkers and superiors to manage expectations and prevent unnecessary overtime.

Take Breaks: Plan frequent breaks throughout your workday. Short pauses help you regain concentration and avoid burnout. Use this opportunity to stretch, go for a stroll, or practice relaxation methods.

Set technological boundaries: To prevent taking up too much of your time, limit your after-work interactions and emails. Make your availability obvious to coworkers and managers.

Delegate and Say No: Learn to delegate duties wherever feasible, and don't be afraid to say no when your plate is full. Overcommitting may cause stress and a lack of work-life balance.

Acknowledge Milestones: Take the time to recognize and celebrate your professional accomplishments. Promotions, completed projects, and personal ambitions are all examples of accomplishments. Celebrating your achievements boosts your feeling of accomplishment.

Gratitude Practice: Begin your gratitude practice by focusing on the good elements of your profession and life. This exercise may improve your general well-being and help you keep a good attitude.

Sharing Successes: Share your successes with friends, family, and coworkers. Celebrating together may foster a feeling of community and increase your pleasure with your successes.

Reward yourself: Consider rewarding yourself after achieving key goals. This might be as easy as treating yourself to a favorite dinner or purchasing a tiny luxury item that you've been wanting. Set new goals. After you've celebrated your successes, create new professional objectives and desires. This keeps you motivated and guarantees that you continue to advance in your chosen career.

Maintaining a work-life balance is an essential component of a rewarding job. Prioritizing self-care, creating clear limits, and recognizing your accomplishments all benefit your general well-being and work happiness.

Remember that a great profession is more than simply moving up the corporate ladder or amassing cash; it is also about living a balanced and meaningful life. By incorporating these ideas into your everyday routine, you may achieve both professional success and a happy, healthy lifestyle. Yours in 'take care of yourself' goodness

CHAPTER 8

Legacy Building: Building For The Future!

You cannot live for yourself. That is short changing yourself. The aim of your life, and the whole idea of existence, is to live a meaningful life that will outlive you. Why? Because this is the way life should be. We'll look at what legacy building is, why it's essential, and how to handle it.

Let's start with a couple of quotes:

If you don't want to be forgotten as soon as you die, either write or do something worthwhile. — Benjamin Franklin

All excellent men and women must take responsibility for leaving legacies that will propel the future generation to heights we can only conceive. – Jim Rohn

Even if your time on the job is limited, if you do a good job, your work will live forever. — Idowu Koyenikan

If you are going to live, leave a legacy. Make an indelible impression on the world. — Maya Angelou Someone is sitting in the shade today as a result of a long-standing tree planting. Warren Buffett

When you hear the word 'legacy', what comes to mind? Inheritance, endowment, settlement, heirloom, gift in trust, etc. It is a term that refers to a person (typically older) leaving something for other people (generally younger), whose lives will be much improved as a result of this gift.

How investing in your legacy can be really powerful and open doors to seats in places you would never have entered otherwise.

One: Determine where your voice can be loudest. Self-discovery is the first step in every construction project. Don't copy and paste because you'll be living in the shadows of others and not being the true you that you were meant to be. If you want to narrow it down to this point, schedule a conversation with me and I will show you how to find your zone of ultimate authenticity.

Two: Begin with the intent to serve, heal, and assist. Legacy building is an important leadership quality, and only great leaders can leave a legacy. True leadership, in this sense, is seeing oneself as someone in the ministry of assistance. When you live your beliefs in front of the people you lead, it becomes easier to model them.

Three: As you serve, look for those who have the skills, aptitude, and talents to complement what you're developing. Listen, some of the individuals you'd directly (or indirectly) mentor and coach may not have the same skill set as you, and that's okay. What matters is that you have what it takes to pour into them in a manner that enhances what they have begun to discover about themselves. You do this via internships, acting as a supervisor (for example, at work), writing, teaching, group and one-on-one sessions. What matters is that you create a system that works for you while also benefiting them to the greatest extent possible.

Four: Provide chances for them to implement what they have learned from you. This stage is critical because it allows you to assess how well you taught them and how well they learned. There will be errors, and you must prepare for them.

This stage is highly important in developing and leaving a legacy since it determines how effectively you raise the individuals who have come to connect with you. This will also translate into chances for them to take off and find their feet/bearing.

Five: Continued progress for you! Recognize the need to invest in yourself and feed as much as you give; otherwise, you will be empty and unable to pour from an empty cup. Legacy building requires time and effort. Your work should not be so difficult to pass on to others. You may want to keep your secret code, but you should pass along the concepts that consistently work and give your mentees the freedom to discover their zone of brilliance. When you raise a leader or help others to become leaders, you are investing in the future.

CHAPTER 9

The Power of Long-Term Financial Planning: Creating a Peaceful and Prosperous Future

Imagine having peace of mind knowing that your financial future is in control. Consider accomplishing your aspirations and goals with security and confidence. Long-term financial planning can offer you this. But, what is it? It is simply the act of identifying objectives and developing a strategy to reach them while using your financial resources effectively and wisely.

Thinking about the future and making choices in the present will take you to the life you want. Why is it important? Long-term financial planning is more than just numbers and spreadsheets; it's about enabling yourself to live the life you want. Taking charge of your money now unlocks a wealth of rewards that go well beyond financial stability.

Here's how.

1. Peace of Mind and Reduced Stress Imagine navigating life's path with the assurance that you're ready for whatever comes your way. Long-term planning allows

you to create a financial buffer, reducing the stress associated with unexpected spending or prospective income interruptions. This peace of mind allows you to concentrate on what is genuinely important, enabling you to enjoy the present moment without always worrying about tomorrow.

2. Goal Achievement: Turning Dreams into Reality Financial ambitions, whether it's a dream trip, a secure retirement, or establishing your own company, might appear remote and unachievable. However, with a defined path developed via long-term planning, these goals become attainable milestones. By identifying your objectives, developing a financial plan, and measuring your progress, you can become the architect of your success, making your aspirations a reality.

3. Freedom and Flexibility: Making Choices on Your Terms. Financial independence is more than simply having enough money; it is about having the flexibility to make decisions that are consistent with your beliefs and goals. Long-term planning enables you to break free from financial limits, enabling you to follow your passions, spend time with loved ones, or embark on life-changing events without financial constraints.

4. Weathering Life's Storms: Developing Resilience Life throws curveballs, and unexpected occurrences such as

job loss, medical problems, or economic downturns may devastate your finances. However, with a strong financial foundation established via long-term preparation, you are better prepared to withstand these storms. Emergency money, diversified assets, and proactive risk management measures serve as safety nets, reducing the effect of unanticipated problems and allowing you to negotiate challenging circumstances more confidently.

5. Maximizing Return on Investment: Increasing Your Wealth Financial planning is more than simply saving; it is about strategically increasing your wealth. By investing sensibly and matching your investments with your long-term objectives, you may use compound interest and outperform inflation. This not only guarantees your future but also enables you to leave a legacy and maybe provide chances for future generations.

To summarize, long-term financial planning is an investment in your future well-being. It enables you to pursue your objectives, overcome obstacles with perseverance, and eventually enjoy a life of freedom, security, and satisfaction.

By taking control of your money now, you prepare the road for a better future, full of opportunities and peace of mind.

How can I get started? Taking charge of your financial future may be difficult, but it can be divided into easy stages.

Here's a guidebook to help you on your journey:

1. Chart Your Course: Define your goals. Imagine yourself in the future. What would your dream life look like? Do you dream of retiring comfortably, exploring the globe, or starting your own business? Identifying your long-term objectives is the first critical step. Set SMART objectives that are precise, measurable, attainable, relevant, and time-bound. This clarity will be your guiding light throughout the planning process.

2. Know Your Numbers: Get a Financial Snapshot Just like a doctor would not give medicine without a diagnosis, you cannot make sound financial choices until you understand your present position. Gather your financial statements, including income sources, monthly spending, and any outstanding obligations. This complete financial survey will highlight your starting place and possible opportunities for change.

3. Make a Budget: Your Roadmap to Saving Consider a budget to be a guide for your expenditures. It assists you in allocating your income between your necessities, desires, and, most importantly, savings and investments. There are several budgeting systems available, so choose one that matches your approach.

Consistency is essential whether using a spreadsheet, a budgeting tool, or the conventional pen-and-paper technique. Track your expenditure for a month to better understand your spending patterns and uncover areas for possible savings. Remember that every dollar saved is an investment in your future.

4. Investigate Your Investment Opportunities: Creating Your Wealth Engine Investing is the key to increasing your money and meeting your long-term objectives. While the world of investing may seem difficult, there are countless solutions to meet various risk tolerances and objectives. Investigate several choices, including fixed income (bonds), equities, investment funds, and even cryptocurrency (with care). Remember, variety is critical. To reduce risk, diversify your assets among asset classes rather than putting all of your eggs in one basket.

5. Adapt and Evolve: Review and Adjust Your Plan Your financial strategy should be dynamic, just as life is. Review your progress regularly and make any necessary

adjustments to your strategy. As your objectives change, your financial approach may need to adjust. Life events, such as a raise, marriage, or starting a family, may affect your income, spending, and investments. Accept flexibility and be willing to fine-tune your strategy to ensure it stays in line with your present situation and future goals. Remember that long-term financial planning is a journey, not a destination. By taking these first actions and keeping dedicated, you'll be well on your way to creating a safe and satisfying future!

Tips for Success:

Start early: The sooner you begin planning, the better. Be disciplined: Sticking to your strategy is vital for attaining your objectives.

Seek knowledge: Learn about money and investing to make better judgments.

Seek expert assistance: A financial adviser may assist you in developing a tailored strategy that meets your specific circumstances. With preparation, dedication, and knowledge, you can create a wealthy and plentiful future for yourself and your family.

www.ingramcontent.com/pod-product-compliance
Lightning Source LLC
Chambersburg PA
CBHW071217240526
45470CB00018B/2066